Pebble Plus

Transportation
in My Neighborhood

by Shelly Lyons

Consulting Editor: Gail Saunders-Smith, PhD

CAPSTONE PRESS
a capstone imprint

Pebble Plus is published by Capstone Press,
1710 Roe Crest Drive, North Mankato, Minnesota 56003.
www.capstonepub.com

Library of Congress Cataloging-in-Publication Data
Lyons, Shelly.
Transportation in my neighborhood / by Shelly Lyons.
p. cm. — (Pebble plus: my neighborhood)
ISBN 978-1-62065-101-8 (library binding)
ISBN 978-1-62065-891-8 (paperback)
ISBN 978-1-4765-1728-5 (ebook PDF)
1. Transportation—Juvenile literature. I. Title.

TA1149.L96 2013
388.4—dc23   2012031091

Editorial Credits
Sarah Bennett, designer; Svetlana Zhurkin, media researcher; Laura Manthe, production specialist

Photo Credits
Alamy: Lightworks Media, 12; Capstone Studio: Karon Dubke, 7; Dreamstime: Shairad, 5; Getty Images: Jan Sonnenmair, 18; iStockphotos: Anna Bryukhanova, 16; Shutterstock: Arena Creative, 11, A-R-T (background), 1 and throughout, Keith Spieldenner, 19, Kzenon, 15, Monkey Business Images, 21, Rafael Ramirez Lee, 17, Stuart Monk, 13, Vacclav, cover; Svetlana Zhurkin, 9

Note to Parents and Teachers

The My Neighborhood set supports social studies standards related to community. This book describes and illustrates transportation in a neighborhood. The images support early readers in understanding the text. The repetition of words and phrases helps early readers learn new words. This book also introduces early readers to subject-specific vocabulary words, which are defined in the Glossary section. Early readers may need assistance to read some words and to use the Table of Contents, Glossary, Read More, Internet Sites, and Index sections of the book.

Printed in the United States of America in North Mankato, Minnesota.
112017   010965R

Table of Contents

What Is Transportation?

Transportation is the way we move from place to place. From cars to trains, we have plenty of ways to travel.

Using Our Legs

Eli and Trent walk home
from school.
Leaves crunch
beneath their feet.

Jess rides her bicycle
to the library.
Brring! She rings the bell
on the handlebar to say hello.

On the Road

Ted rides in the car

with his grandma.

The traffic on the highway

crawls and stops,

crawls and stops.

Gina and her mom find a taxi.

Gina asks the driver

to take them to the museum.

13

Shana and her aunt ride
the bus to the movies.
Shana will slide her card
into the reader.

card reader

Tracks and Waves

Sam and his aunt ride
the subway to visit Grandma.
The train winds through
the dark tunnel.

Justin and his mom take

a ferry to an island.

They park the car below deck.

Neighborhoods have many different kinds of transportation. How do you like to get around?

Glossary

deck—a floor-like surface that stretches across different levels of a ship

ferry—a boat that carries people across a stretch of water

highway—a main road that connects towns or cities

island—a piece of land that is surrounded by water

neighborhood—a small area in a town or city where people live

reader—a machine that takes in a bus card and charges the rider a fee

subway—a system of trains that runs underground in a city

traffic—vehicles that are moving on a road

transportation—a way to move from one place to another

Read More

Gaarder-Juntti, Oona. *What in the World Is Green Transportation?* Going Green. Edina, Minn.: ABDO Pub. Company, 2011.

Salas, Laura Purdie. *Always Got My Feet: Poems about Transportation*. Poetry. Mankato, Minn.: Capstone Press, 2009.

Spengler, Kremena. *An Illustrated Timeline of Transportation*. Visual Timelines in History. Mankato, Minn.: Picture Window Books, 2012.

Internet Sites

FactHound offers a safe, fun way to find Internet sites related to this book. All of the sites on FactHound have been researched by our staff.

Here's all you do:

Visit *www.facthound.com*

Type in this code: 9781620651018

Super-cool stuff!

Check out projects, games and lots more at
www.capstonekids.com

Index

Word Count: 152
Grade: 1
Early-Intervention Level: 16